Faith and action

DR PETER SAUNDERS

Copyright © The Christian Institute 2016

The author has asserted his right under Section 77 of the Copyright, Designs & Patents Act 1988 to be identified as the author of this work.

Printed in October 2016

ISBN 978-1-901086-56-0

Jointly published by:
The Christian Institute, Wilberforce House, 4 Park Road, Gosforth Business Park, Newcastle upon Tyne, NE12 8DG; and
Christian Medical Fellowship, 6 Marshalsea Road, London, SE1 1HL

All rights reserved

No part of this publication may be reproduced, or stored in a retrieval system, or transmitted, in any form or by any means, mechanical, electronic, photocopying, recording or otherwise, without the prior permission of The Christian Institute.

All scripture quotations, unless otherwise indicated, are taken from the HOLY BIBLE, NEW INTERNATIONAL VERSION®. NIV®. Copyright © 1973, 1978, 1984 by International Bible Society. Used by permission of Zondervan. All rights reserved.

The Christian Institute is a Company Limited by Guarantee, registered in England as a charity. Company No. 263 4440, Charity No. 100 4774. A charity registered in Scotland. Charity No. SC039220

Christian Medical Fellowship is a Company Limited by Guarantee, registered in England no. 6949436. Registered Charity no. 1131658.

Contents

5   Foreword

7   Truth under attack

13   The new liberalism

17   The new conservativism

21   Repentance and faith

27   Our high calling

> For it is by grace you have been saved, through faith—and this not from yourselves, it is the gift of God—not by works, so that no-one can boast. For we are God's workmanship, created in Christ Jesus to do good works, which God prepared in advance for us to do.

EPHESIANS 2:8-10

> What good is it, my brothers, if a man claims to have faith but has no deeds? Can such faith save him? Suppose a brother or sister is without clothes and daily food. If one of you says to him, 'Go, I wish you well; keep warm and well fed,' but does nothing about his physical needs, what good is it? In the same way, faith by itself, if it is not accompanied by action, is dead. But someone will say, 'You have faith; I have deeds.' Show me your faith without deeds, and I will show you my faith by what I do.

JAMES 2:14-18

Foreword

At the beginning of the twenty-first century we are facing unprecedented ethical challenges, especially in the areas of sexuality and end-of-life decision-making.

One would expect that Christians who accept the Bible as their sole and sufficient authority would be bold and clear in responding to these challenges. Not so, argues Dr Peter Saunders. All too often there is a reluctance to speak out. Conservative evangelicals may be bold when it comes to defending the 'central' doctrines of salvation but timid when it comes to speaking out on ethical issues.

In this lecture, delivered in Newcastle upon Tyne in November 2013, Peter Saunders explains why. He speaks of a new liberal heresy, which filters difficult ethical questions through a simplistic grid of 'love' or 'compassion'. This, in effect, can neutralise biblical calls to obedience. He also warns against a new conservative heresy, which regards an emphasis on ethics as 'legalistic' and a 'distraction from the gospel of grace'.

Positively, Dr Saunders points to Christ's call to repentance and faith. We cannot afford to neglect either doctrine or ethics. Faith without works is dead.

We hope and pray that this booklet will reaffirm the Christian's calling to be courageous in obedience, out of love for God and for the good of all.

Colin Hart
Director, The Christian Institute

Truth under attack

> " *If I profess with the loudest voice and clearest exposition every portion of the Word of God except precisely that little point which the world and the devil are at that moment attacking, I am not confessing Christ, however boldly I may be professing Him. Where the battle rages there the loyalty of the soldier is proved; and to be steady on all the battle front besides, is mere flight and disgrace if he flinches at that point.* "

This famous quote has been attributed to Martin Luther by Christian commentators as illustrious as Francis Schaeffer but, as argued convincingly by Carl Wieland, it actually comes from a nineteenth century novel referring to Luther by Elizabeth Rundle Charles called *The Chronicles of the Schoenberg Cotta Family* (Thomas Nelson, 1864).

However, according to Wieland, Luther did say something very similar. He said that if people were publicly open about every other aspect of their Christian faith, but chose not to admit their belief on some single point of doctrine (for fear of what might happen to them if their conviction on that one point became known) they were effectively denying Christ, period.

As Christians we are fighting in a spiritual battle, but Martin Luther's point is that not all God's truth is equally under attack at any one time. In any culture and generation there are certain truths which are more under attack than others.

As Christians in twenty-first century Britain we need to be aware of which Christian truth is most under attack, and ensure that we are faithful in standing for that truth.

There are some worthy causes that in Britain today are politically correct. If you campaign, for example, to end child poverty, to care for trees in the Amazon rainforest, to fight cancer, to clamp down on loan sharks, or to curb human trafficking, you will find yourself in a large like-minded company of both believers and unbelievers.

This does not mean that these are not important causes for which Christians should fight. They are. But my point is that few if any will publicly oppose you for making a stand on them. Especially in the church, you will find many allies who will stand alongside you.

It's terribly important that Christians and churches, particularly at a time of economic recession, are moving into areas like food bank provision, debt counselling and street pastoring. The needs are great and we should be involved.

But if we restrict ourselves to those areas of Christian service that our society applauds, then we are being selective in our discipleship. Luther might even say we are denying Christ.

Most unbelievers are very accepting of Christians who support popular causes and it is tempting to imagine that if we are being good and faithful Christians everyone will like us. Jesus said exactly the opposite (Matthew 10:22; John 16:1-3).

The Bible reminds us that everyone who genuinely seeks to live a godly life in Christ will be persecuted in one way or another (2 Timothy 3:12). It was the false prophets, Jesus said, of whom everyone spoke well (Luke 6:26). We must ensure that our only offence is that of the gospel, but often in the Christian walk opposition is a sign that we are doing a good job rather than a bad job.

Many people hated Jesus simply because he spoke truth that people did not want to hear (John 7:7; 15:18) – that is precisely why he was crucified. Likewise when we speak the same truth some people will dislike us, and perhaps even hate us too.

Persecution began for the early church when Peter, John and Stephen opened their mouths and started to speak (see Acts 5:17-42; 6:9-10). We must of course speak the truth in love (Ephesians 4:15), but how often do we use 'sensitivity' simply as an excuse for cowardice, when our real underlying motive is to avoid being persecuted for the cross of Christ? (Galatians 6:12)

The high-profile cases involving Christians getting into trouble with the law or governing authorities in Britain, with which we are all familiar, tend to involve a limited number of issues. Homosexuality is a particularly common theme – whether it is a couple running a bed and breakfast who wish to ensure their clientele sharing a double room are married, or street preachers addressing moral issues, or a housing officer commenting on a personal Facebook page.

When it comes to Christian doctors being hauled up before their NHS trusts, or being complained about to the General Medical Council, or being the subject of court proceedings, it is similarly a small number of issues that tend to feature.

If a Christian doctor wishes to opt out of abortion or being a medical advisor on gay adoption, or expresses views about these issues, or attempts to pray with or share the gospel with a patient or colleague, there are risks of losing one's reputation, job or even licence to practise.

If you publicly express biblical views on subjects like abortion, euthanasia or sex you can become very unpopular indeed. In 2012, in response to direct questioning on Twitter, I expressed in simple terms what I regard to be an orthodox Christian view of sex. I said, "All people are sinners and also all sex outside marriage is morally wrong" and "Sex between two people of the same sex - male or female - is always wrong".

My responses were then retweeted by an atheist doctor (who was also gay) to several thousand of his followers and I was buried for several hours under a barrage of the most unpleasant abuse you can possibly imagine.

I was recently out for a meal with a friend, with whom I have a fair degree in common, who told me that he disagreed with me about three things. While I was inwardly shaking my head with astonishment at 'only three' (!) my friend informed me that the three things in question were abortion, assisted suicide and homosexual practice.

My own view, as you might guess, is that abortion, assisted suicide and homosexual practice are not good ideas.

But the friend in question, an evangelical Christian theologian and Bible college lecturer, felt strongly that there was a place for Christian involvement in all three. These views are not unusual.

The Evangelical Alliance surveyed 17,000 'evangelicals', mainly at conferences like New Wine and Spring Harvest, in 2010 and published the results in January 2011. Amongst the questions was one on each of abortion, assisted suicide and homosexuality. A wide range of views were expressed:

- *63% of British evangelicals did not agree that abortion can never be justified;*
- *40% did not agree that assisted suicide is always wrong;*
- *27% did not agree that homosexual actions are always wrong.*

Remember that these are conference-going evangelicals and probably represent, therefore, a relatively committed section of the evangelical population.

The Richard Dawkins Foundation for Reason and Science (UK) found in a poll published in 2012 that of those who called themselves Christians:[1]

- *62% favoured a woman's right to have an abortion within the legal time limit;*
- *46% did not disapprove of sexual relations between two adults of the same sex;*
- *23% believed that sex between a man and a woman was only acceptable within marriage;*
- *74% believed that religion should not influence public policy.*

Why is it that so many Christians now have views on these issues that would have been considered anathema just a generation ago?

First, and perhaps obviously, the prevailing culture has shifted hugely on these questions. The so-called mountains of culture – Parliament, universities, institutions, law, science, media, arts, entertainment – are increasingly dominated by people with an atheistic worldview. This new 'liberal elite' believes that God doesn't exist, that death is the end and that morality is relative to each individual. But in practice most adopt the ethics of secular humanism. Undoubtedly this cultural change has affected the church.

Second, as I have already alluded to, taking a traditional view on these issues now carries a cost that it did not have a generation ago. In 2012, Christians in Parliament, an official All-Party Parliamentary Group (APPG) chaired by Gary Streeter MP, launched an inquiry called 'Clearing the Ground', which was tasked with considering the question: 'Are Christians marginalised in the UK?' Its main conclusion was that, "Christians in the UK face problems in living out their faith and these problems have been mostly caused and exacerbated by social, cultural and legal changes over the past decade." There is loss of reputation, job and income to consider with certain Christian beliefs and behaviours.

Third, some Christian leaders with large followings have changed their position on these issues. The Bishop of Liverpool, James Jones, and baptist minister Steve Chalke are two examples of prominent Christian leaders who came out in 2013 in support of the church affirming monogamous gay (sexual) partnerships. There is intense speculation that the Church of England's Pilling Report is about to be published recommending the same thing.[2]

Fourth, there has been a huge decline in Bible reading and study generally, and in Bible teaching specifically. In particular, there is very little teaching in our churches about ethical issues. This year I was asked, for the very first time in 20 years of ministry with CMF, to lead a seminar on abortion at a leading conservative evangelical church in London. We were told that it was being widely advertised through home groups and by the over 30 full-time workers in a congregation of more than 1,000. Twelve people turned up. I learnt later that the poor attendance was due to the fact that the leadership had not thought it important enough to advertise. Last week I was asked by the editor of a major denomination's ministers' magazine to write an article on the biblical case against euthanasia. He was concerned that many ministers in his (well-known) Bible-believing denomination were of the view that euthanasia in hard cases was a genuine act of Christian mercy.

But, whilst these four factors play a part in accounting for what I would call ethical drift amongst Christians, I think the real reasons are more deeply theological. I would attribute them to two destructive wrong beliefs (dare I say heresies?) – one infecting liberal evangelical congregations and one infecting conservative evangelical ones. In both groups are many who know their Bibles very well, but who are increasingly adopting ethical views that are much closer to that of the prevailing culture than those held historically by the church.

Let's look at each of these in turn. I'll call them the new liberalism and the new conservativism, although, as we will see, neither of them are, in reality, new.

---

[1] Ipsos MORI poll, *Religious and Social Attitudes of UK Christians in 2011*, 14 Feb 2012, see https://www.ipsos-mori.com/researchpublications/researcharchive/2921/Religious-and-Social-Attitudes-of-UK-Christians-in-2011.aspx as at 20 September 2016

[2] The 'Pilling Report', published on 28 November 2013, recommended that gay unions should be marked by special church services. See http://www.christian.org.uk/news/churches-should-mark-gay-unions-says-c-of-e-report/ as at 20 September 2016

The new liberalism

The old liberalism had its roots in the radical biblical criticism of the nineteenth century. Old liberals doubted core Christian doctrines like the incarnation, Christ's death and resurrection, his ascension and second coming, the authority of Scripture, justification by faith, the day of judgment and the sovereignty of God.

The new liberalism is orthodox on these things. New liberals will gladly tick the boxes of the church creeds and the doctrinal basis of the Evangelical Alliance and they know their Bibles well. They are liberal not on what we might call the core beliefs of Christianity, but on ethics. They would argue that ethical issues are in the category of what Paul called "disputable matters" – see passages like Romans 14 and 1 Corinthians 8 and 10.

Disputable matters are things on which Bible-believing Christians can legitimately disagree whilst remaining in fellowship with one another. They are in the same category as debates about the timing and amount of water to be used in baptism, how often the Lord's Supper is celebrated, the sequence of events around the return of Christ, forms of church government and the place of Israel.

I see the new liberalism as a revival of what in a previous generation was called 'situation ethics'.

Situation ethics is a 'Christian' ethical theory that was principally developed in the 1960s by the then Episcopal priest Joseph Fletcher. Fletcher (1905-1991) taught Christian Ethics at Episcopal Theological School, Cambridge, Massachusetts, and at the University of Virginia. He wrote ten books and hundreds of articles, book reviews, and translations.

Situation ethics basically states that other moral principles can be cast aside in certain situations if love is best served. As theologian Paul Tillich once put it: "Love is the ultimate law". The moral principles Fletcher was specifically referring to were the moral codes of Christianity and the type of love he was specifically referring to is 'agape' love.

Fletcher believed that in forming an ethical system based on love, he was best expressing the notion of 'love thy neighbour', which Jesus Christ taught in the Gospels. He believed that there are no absolute laws other than the law of 'agape' love, meaning that all the other laws are only guidelines on how to achieve this love, and could be broken if an alternative course of action would result in more love. In order to establish his thesis he employed a number of famous examples of 'situations' in which it might be justified to administer euthanasia, commit adultery, steal, tell a lie, etc – what we might call 'hard cases'.

But in effectively divorcing 'agape' love from moral law, Fletcher was steering a subtly different path from Jesus himself.

Jesus did indeed say (Matthew 22:34-40) that the most important commands in the Old Testament Law were love of God and neighbour (Deuteronomy 6:5 and Leviticus 19:18). In fact he said these two commandments summed up the whole of Old Testament Law (Matthew 22:40 and Luke 10:25-28). Furthermore he criticised the Pharisees for obeying the less important parts of the law (tithing mint and cumin) whilst neglecting the "more important matters of... justice, mercy and faithfulness" (Matthew 23:23).

But he also said that "Anyone who breaks one of the least of these commandments and teaches others to do the same will be called least in the kingdom of heaven" (Matthew 5:19) and reproved the Pharisees by saying that they should have "practised the latter" (important commandments) "without neglecting the former" (lesser commandments).

Certainly there is no place in the Gospels where Jesus implies that those commandments which deal with the shedding of innocent blood and sexual immorality (numbers six and seven of the Ten Commandments) should be disobeyed.

By contrast he exhorts his disciples in the Sermon on the Mount to go beyond the mere legalities of "you shall not murder" and "you shall not commit adultery" to embody the very spirit of love which undergirds them. Not only no murder or adultery but no hate or lust either! (Matthew 5:21-30).

It is this more exacting moral standard that also underlies the ethical teaching in the epistles. Christians are exhorted to be imitators of Christ (1 Corinthians 11:1) and God (Ephesians 5:1-2), to walk as Christ walked (1 John 2:6) and to "abstain from sinful desires" (1 Peter 2:11).

In short we are to live by "Christ's law" (1 Corinthians 9:21 and Galatians 6:2) and to love one another as he has loved us (John 13:34-35). And love of Jesus involves obedience to Jesus (John 14:15, 21 and 15:12). In fact Jesus famously answered one of the Devil's temptations in the wilderness by quoting from Deuteronomy, "Man does not live on bread alone, but on *every word* that comes from the mouth of God" (Matthew 4:4). Note *every* word.

So whilst we may say that there are situations where choosing not to shed innocent blood or to carry out a sexually immoral act requires great grace, courage, restraint and self-sacrifice, there are no situations where one may choose to murder or to do something sexually immoral and claim to be acting in love.

If Christ had been directly tempted in such a way, and indeed he must have been if he was "tempted in every way, just as we are" as we are told he was (Hebrews 4:15), we can imagine him answering as he did in the wilderness, "It is written, 'you shall not murder', 'you shall not commit adultery'".

I am not suggesting in any of this that Christians are still under the Old Covenant made with the nation of Israel (Exodus 19:4-6). There is now a new sacrifice, a new priesthood and a new law. Christ inaugurated a New Covenant (Luke 22:20), as promised by the prophets (Jeremiah 31:31-34; Ezekiel 36:24-32), and explained by the apostles (Galatians 3:2-14; Hebrews 8:1-13, 10:1-18). As described above, although we are not under 'the law', we are certainly not thereby free from moral constraint. Rather we are under "Christ's law", which is far more exacting in its moral demands.

The Old Covenant was prophetic in the sense that it pointed to Christ as its fulfilment. But the New Covenant has a far more profound moral dimension than the Old, because we are called not just to conform to a set of laws but to be, by God's grace, imitators of Christ and of God himself.

By my reading situation ethics is a distortion of biblical ethical teaching. It is, in short, heresy. But it is a heresy that appears to be very much alive and well amongst more liberal British evangelicals in the twenty-first century.

Interestingly, Fletcher later identified himself as an atheist and was active in the Euthanasia Society of America and the American Eugenics Society, and was one of the signatories to the Humanist Manifesto. When he started out, his position was barely distinguishable from orthodoxy. But he finished up in a very different place altogether. This is exactly what happens when we define 'love' in a different way from the way it is defined in the Bible.

The new conservativism

The new conservatives are suspicious of ethics for another reason. They think that an emphasis on ethics undermines grace and distracts from the preaching of the gospel. They also fear that it leads to legalism.

They want to place emphasis, quite rightly, on the fact that salvation is a gift that we cannot earn. Salvation is through God's grace alone and received by faith alone.

> " For it is by grace you have been saved, through faith—and this not from yourselves, it is the gift of God—not by works, so that no-one can boast. " (Ephesians 2:8-9)

> " [We] know that a man is not justified by observing the law, but by faith in Jesus Christ. So we, too, have put our faith in Christ Jesus that we may be justified by faith in Christ and not by observing the law, because by observing the law no-one will be justified. " (Galatians 2:16)

These of course are some of the great biblical truths rediscovered by the Reformers, and all of us would say to them a hearty 'Amen'.

But my concern is that if we emphasise this aspect of salvation without reference to the rest of Scripture we risk an imbalance in the opposite direction.

Now first, let me dispel any doubt that I am in any way attempting to undermine the absolute centrality of the cross and the doctrine of substitutionary atonement or penal substitution.

The idea of substitutionary atonement, that Christ died in our place for our sins, is absolutely central to both Old Testament and New Testament.

It underlies the Passover, the Jewish sacrificial system, temple worship and the Day of Atonement and is perhaps nowhere spelt out more clearly than in Isaiah 53, the last of the four servant songs, written 700 years before Christ was crucified and in anticipation of it:

> " Surely he **took up our infirmities** and **carried our sorrows**... But he was **pierced for our transgressions**, he was **crushed for our iniquities**; the **punishment that brought us peace was upon him**, and **by his wounds we are healed**... and **the Lord has laid on him the iniquity of us all.** " (Isaiah 53:4-6)

Later in the chapter we are told that the Servant (Jesus) was "led like a lamb to the slaughter", "for the transgression of my people he was stricken", "the Lord makes his life a guilt offering", "my righteous servant will justify many", "he will bear their iniquities", "he bore the sin of many".

In the same way substitutionary atonement is the central teaching of the New Testament.

Paul teaches that Jesus died "for us" (Romans 5:6-8; 2 Corinthians 5:14; 1 Thessalonians 5:10) and also that he died "for our sins" (1 Corinthians 15:3; Galatians 1:4).

Jesus describes his own ministry as giving his life "as a ransom for many" (Matthew 20:28; Mark 10:45) and Peter says "He himself bore our sins in his body on the tree" (1 Peter 2:24). Christ, Paul tells Timothy, "gave himself as a ransom for all men" (1 Timothy 2:6). The writer of Hebrews adds that Christ "died as a ransom to set them free from the sins committed under the first covenant" (Hebrews 9:15). Peter sums it up in saying that "Christ died for sins once for all, the righteous for the unrighteous, to bring you to God" (1 Peter 3:18).

To further unpack this theme the New Testament explains substitutionary atonement with four main metaphors.

- First is the metaphor of the **altar of sacrifice**. Christ is the **sacrificial lamb** whose blood is shed in our place. It is we who deserved to die but Christ substituted himself instead (e.g. Hebrews 7:27).
- Second is the **slave market**. Christ paid the **redemption** price that we could not pay in order to free us from bondage. He bore the cost for us (e.g. 1 Peter 1:18).
- Third is the **law court**. Christ is our **justification**, that is, he took the punishment that we deserved in order that we might not be condemned (e.g. Romans 8:1).
- Fourth is the metaphor of **relationship**. Christ's death on our behalf brings **reconciliation** after our unilateral abandonment of God (e.g. 2 Corinthians 5:18-19).

Like any metaphor, each of these illustrations provides a picture of what actually happened when Jesus died on the cross in our place. In each case he did what we, in our weakness and sin, were unable to do and he did it for, and in place of, us (Romans 5:6-8). Jesus through dying on the cross took the wrath and judgment that our sins deserved; and because he has taken that wrath and judgment in our place we receive mercy and are thereby forgiven.

These things are all givens, the foundation from which we start. But my real concern is that in emphasising 'grace' conservative British evangelicals have fallen into what the German war-time Christian martyr Dietrich Bonhoeffer termed "cheap grace", in his book *The Cost of Discipleship*.

I read this book as a teenager and it had a profound effect on me. Bonhoeffer writes:

> 66 Cheap grace is the grace we bestow on ourselves. Cheap grace is the preaching of forgiveness without requiring repentance, baptism without church discipline, Communion without confession.... Cheap grace is grace without discipleship, grace without the cross, grace without Jesus Christ, living and incarnate 99.

But what does this cheap grace look like? Bonhoeffer points especially to two things that mark out cheap grace from real grace:

- *Cheap grace is without repentance;*
- *Cheap grace is a grace we bestow on ourselves, in other words, it is a grace we give each other when we see fit, rather than according to the pattern of God.*

It's my conviction that the current misunderstanding about grace amongst some evangelicals results from a lack of understanding of the true nature of repentance and faith. Furthermore, this misunderstanding of the true nature of repentance and faith is built on a failure to appreciate the holiness of God, the seriousness of sin and the necessity of judgment.

This also explains many evangelicals' discomfort with the kind of questions the new atheists are raising about the character of God in questions around the problem of suffering, the eternal destiny of unbelievers and God's acts of judgment in the Old Testament. If questions about the slaughter of the Amorites, for example, make us feel uncomfortable, it may be that we have not yet properly understood holiness, sin and judgment.

Scripture tells us that both repentance and faith are themselves gifts of God's grace – he enables us to repent and have faith because we are incapable of doing it on our own (Acts 5:31; 2 Timothy 2:25). But what is the nature of this repentance and faith?

Repentance and faith

Repentance is much more than saying sorry, or even being genuinely remorseful about our sin. It involves an active turning from sin to obedience. We leave our former life behind and follow in Jesus' footsteps. He becomes our Lord and master. Furthermore it is a lifelong orientation; an ongoing, lifelong turning from sin in response to God's Word. The parable of the sower is not just about conversion – it addresses our ongoing lifelong response to God's Word. It's not just about starting off well, but persevering through both hardship and temptation.

John the Baptist, at the beginning of his public ministry in Luke 3, tells those who come to be baptised by him to: "Produce fruit in keeping with repentance" (v8). When they ask him what he means, he outlines specific steps of obedience that they must take. He tells the crowd, "The man with two tunics should share with him who has none, and the one who has food should do the same" (v11). He says to the tax collectors, "Don't collect any more than you are required to" (v13). He tells the soldiers, "Don't extort money and don't accuse people falsely—be content with your pay" (v14).

Jesus takes the same approach: to the rich young ruler, "sell everything you have and give to the poor" (Luke 18:22); to the healed cripple by the pool of Bethesda, "Stop sinning or something worse may happen to you" (John 5:14); to the woman caught in the act of adultery, "leave your life of sin" (John 8:11). To say sorry, and to then continue in sin, is not repentance. It is presumption.

In the same way, faith is more than mere belief, mere intellectual assent to a doctrinal checklist. It is trusting obedience. James tells us that even demons believe – and shudder (James 2:19). Demons, however, do not possess saving faith. They do not trust and obey.

As evangelicals we are quick to assert that we are saved by faith alone, but in fact the only verse in the Bible which uses the two words 'faith' and 'alone' together (James 2:24) appears at first to say the very opposite:

> " *You see that a person is justified by what he does and not by faith alone* ".

Of course this does not mean in any sense that we contribute something to our salvation. We are powerless to do anything to save ourselves, but nonetheless the evidence of genuine saving faith is a changed life – actions. James gives us the examples of Abraham and Rahab who demonstrated the genuineness of their faith by what they did.

They were, we are told, "considered righteous" for what they did (James 2:21 and 25). If we were in any doubt, James summarises it for us, "faith without deeds is dead" (v26).

The faith heroes of Hebrews 11, held up to us as examples, all demonstrated their faith through what they did: Abel offered a sacrifice, Noah built an ark, Abraham left his home, Joseph gave instructions about his bones, Moses refused to be known as the son of Pharaoh's daughter, Rahab welcomed the spies, Gideon conquered kingdoms, and so on. Each one demonstrated their faith by what they did and they did these things at considerable personal risk.

The Apostle Paul's letters illustrate the same principle. They are full of ethical instruction: 'Because these things are true about Christ and his work, therefore do this, and don't do that.' That is the pattern in virtually every epistle. He speaks to the Thessalonians of their "work produced by faith" and their "labour prompted by love" (1 Thessalonians 1:3). He prays that the Colossians will bear fruit "in every good work" (Colossians 1:10). He exhorts Timothy to watch *both* his life and his doctrine closely (1 Timothy 4:16) and tells Titus that Jesus gave himself for us "to redeem us from all wickedness and to purify for himself a people that are his very own, *eager to do what is good*" (Titus 2:14).

He tells the Romans that they are called to *"the obedience that comes from faith"* (Romans 1:5; see also 16:26).

The books that most emphasise that we are saved by grace through faith – Galatians and Ephesians, which we quoted from earlier – also demonstrate that this faith is evidenced by good works.

In Galatians we are told that: "The only thing that counts is faith *expressing itself through love*" (Galatians 5:6). Not a feeling, but an action. Ephesians tells us that we are saved by grace and not by works, but that we are "created in Christ Jesus *to do good works*, which God prepared in advance for us to do" (Ephesians 2:8-10).

The Apostle John tells us in his first epistle that those who continue to sin have neither seen Christ nor known him (1 John 3:6).

The Apostle Peter exhorts his readers: "As obedient children, do not conform to the evil desires you had when you lived in ignorance. But just as he who called you is holy, so be holy in all you do; for it is written: 'Be holy, because I am holy'" (1 Peter 1:14-16).

Nowhere is this principle of obedient trust more evident than in the Gospels themselves. Jesus says that to those who call him "Lord" but *do not do* his Father's will, he will say "I never knew you" (Matthew 7:21-23). The difference between the man who built his house on the sand and the other who built it on the rock is this: both heard Jesus' words but only one *'put them into practice'* (Matthew 7:24-27). The exacting commands of the Sermon on the Mount, going as they do right to our innermost heart and motivations, are intended to be *obeyed*. They are not there solely to convict us of sin.

Obedience to Christ is of course only possible by God's grace, through the indwelling work of his Holy Spirit, but Christians are nonetheless called to obey him. In fact the heart of the Great Commission, sadly so often distorted into an exhortation merely to evangelise, is to "make disciples of all nations... *teaching them to obey everything* I have commanded you" (Matthew 28:19-20).

God intends us to grow into full maturity. Consistent with this the writer of Hebrews calls his readers to leave aside what he calls "the elementary teachings about Christ and go on to maturity". They are instead to become acquainted with "the teaching about righteousness" and by taking "solid food", 'train themselves to distinguish good from evil' (Hebrews 5:11-6:3). It is about actions; trusting obedience as the evidence of genuine faith.

As a clear corollary of this teaching we are told that a life without demonstrable evidence of faith through a changed life is valueless. It is evidence of non-regeneration.

Galatians 5:19-21 warns that those who exhibit the "acts of the sinful nature" – "sexual immorality, impurity and debauchery; idolatry and witchcraft; hatred, discord, jealousy, fits of rage, selfish ambition, dissensions, factions and envy; drunkenness, orgies, and the like" – *"will not inherit the kingdom of God"*.

In like manner 1 Corinthians 6:9-10 tells us: "Neither the sexually immoral nor idolaters nor adulterers nor male prostitutes nor homosexual offenders nor thieves nor the greedy nor drunkards nor slanderers nor swindlers *will inherit the kingdom of God"*.

The book of Revelation (20:12) tells us that the dead will be 'judged *according to what they have done'*. In case we are in any doubt, it adds that "the cowardly, the unbelieving, the vile, *the murderers, the sexually immoral*, those who practise magic arts, the idolaters and all liars – their place will be in the fiery lake of burning sulphur" (21:8). Outside the holy city will be "those who practise magic arts, *the sexually immoral, the murderers*, the idolaters and everyone who loves and practises falsehood" (22:15); they will not partake of the tree of life.

The book of Hebrews (10:26-27) tells us that: "If we deliberately keep on sinning after we have received the knowledge of the truth, no sacrifice for sins is left, but only a fearful expectation of judgment and of raging fire that will consume the enemies of God."

These are very serious warnings indeed, and I think they underline the even greater seriousness of false teaching that leads people astray and does not confront them with this truth.

Jesus, for example, calls the church of Thyatira to repentance over 'tolerating that woman Jezebel' who 'by her teaching' "misleads my servants into sexual immorality" (Revelation 2:20-25).

Sex outside marriage is viewed very seriously in Scripture but false teaching which leads people into sexual sin is viewed even more seriously (Luke 17:1-2) and warnings about the affirmation and endorsement of sexual immorality – 2 Peter 2 and Jude are poignant examples – are particularly strong.

Those who lead "little ones" astray (Matthew 18:6), like those they mislead, are in great danger. This is why it is so important for us to exercise godly discipline of such people within our churches (Matthew 18:15-20; Luke 17:3-4; Galatians 6:1; James 5:19-20) for their own sakes, as well as for those whom they might mislead or have already misled.

Those who raise these uncomfortable issues in the church are often told 'not to judge', but the Bible is very clear that in the case of sexual immorality or false teaching it is actually our responsibility as Christians to exercise discipline (1 Corinthians 5:1-13). It is disobedience not to do so. It is one of the marks of a biblical church that there is willingness, where necessary, to exercise such discipline.

I began by making reference to the issues of abortion, euthanasia and homosexual behaviour and the wide variety of views that exist about them in the evangelical church in Britain. I perhaps could have said similar things about covetousness, self-absorption, pornography, overeating, cowardice, jealousy, drunkenness or lack of generosity – other sins which are arguably endemic in British churches but seldom addressed from the pulpit.

But there is something particularly pernicious about the triad of idolatry, sexual immorality and the shedding of innocent blood. These were the particular besetting sins of the nations Israel displaced from the Promised Land and they were the specific sins that led to Israel's own downfall.

Judah fell to Babylon ultimately, we are told, because King Manasseh "had filled Jerusalem with innocent blood, and the LORD was not willing to forgive" (2 Kings 24:4). How, it might be asked, does God view a nation like Britain which has presided over eight million abortions?

We are told uniquely, "Flee from sexual immorality" because it is a sin against a person's "own body" (1 Corinthians 6:18-20). Being sanctified involves avoiding sexual immorality (1 Thessalonians 4:3).

But Romans 1 tells us that both sexual immorality and the shedding of innocent blood have their roots in idolatry. And Francis Schaeffer perceptively said that the idols of the West are "personal peace" and "affluence". One might add the radical pursuit of personal autonomy – that sense of entitlement we exhibit – as another idol in the West. Given that our idols are what we most desire, it is a small step, which we sadly do not have time to unpack now, to see how both sexual immorality and the shedding of innocent blood have their roots in our relentless pursuit of affluence and personal peace, in other words, a life unencumbered by the burden of caring for others. Anything that stands in the way of achieving these goals – be it sexual fidelity, unborn children or dependent relatives – can be legitimately sacrificed.

All of this should drive us back to the foot of the cross, to the one who gave everything to reconcile us to God, and who calls us to carry his cross today; accepting joyfully the suffering and ridicule a life of genuine repentance and trusting obedience brings – being faithful to the hard truths as well as the easier ones.

Our high calling

So what can we say by way of conclusion about our calling as Christians?

We are called as Christians to walk in the footsteps of Jesus Christ, to be holy, to be imitators of God, to live a life of love.

We are called to be obedient not just in those areas where the world applauds us, but also in those where we arouse its hostility.

We are called to an obedience that surpasses the mere legalities of the Old Covenant, to fulfil the very spirit of New Covenant love of which they are a mere shadow.

We are called not to embrace a cheap grace, without repentance and self-bestowed, but to receive God's costly grace that only he can give.

We are called to a repentance that doesn't just say sorry but actively turns from sin.

We are called to a faith that is not mere intellectual assent but trusting, costly obedience.

We are called to carry the cross – to bear one another's burdens and to love one another as he has loved us – because this is the law of Christ (Galatians 6:2; John 13:34-35).

We are called to live holy and godly lives – lives set apart to show his character and display his fruit – as we look forward to the day of God and speed its coming (2 Peter 3:12).

We are called to all these things by the one who did not consider equality with God something to be grasped, but made himself nothing, taking the very nature of a servant, being made in human likeness, and became obedient to death on a cross, that we might be reconciled to him for all eternity (Philippians 2:6-11).